2-00
9/22

OFFSIDE!

Contemporary Artists and Football

OFFSIDE!
Contemporary Artists and Football

ADAM BEEBEE

RODERICK BUCHANAN

FREDDY CONTRERAS

ROSANA FUERTES

LUCY GUNNING

CRISTIN JONES

GABRIEL

DAVID MACH

SIMON PATTERSON

NATALIE TURNER

MARTIN VINCENT

MARK WALLINGER

NICK WAPLINGTON

Manchester City Art
Galleries
Institute of International
Visual Arts

In 1966 preliminary games for the World Cup were held in Manchester and the City Art Galleries mounted an accompanying exhibition of art inspired by the 'many manifestations' of English football 'from the impromptu game in the park and the rough-and-tumble of the village team to the more sophisticated events at Stamford Bridge or Maine Road'. Most of the paintings and sculptures were figurative celebrating 'the climax of the scored goal and the involvement of the fans in the fortunes of their teams'. Whatever one may now think of the then director's assessment of which were the most advanced clubs in English football, there is no doubt that both football and art have undergone radical changes in the thirty years since then. Both are now bound up in complicated ways with the tourist, marketing and leisure industries and both have reached out to broader and more knowledgeable audiences than ever before.

Manchester City Art Galleries had been planning to mount another exhibition on the theme of football for some time now and Howard Smith and Tim Wilcox were already working on it when the opportunity arose to invite John Gill to select an exhibition on this theme. The Institute of International Visual Arts was delighted to accept Manchester City Art Galleries' invitation to collaborate on this exhibition which reflects the Institute's desire to make contemporary art more accessible to a wider public and, at the same time, to explore the ways in which our national game reflects our image of ourselves, our nation and our relationship with other nations. Both of our organisations have enjoyed and profited from collaborating on this exhibition which we hope will be a source of enjoyment and interest to visitors. Its prepartion has coincided with the development of the SoccerCity Festival of Art and Sport which has been put together by Manchester City Council to enhance the staging of the European Football Championships in Manchester and we are very pleased to be playing a major part in the festival. Our thanks are due to Jane Bateman, Colin Sinclair of Castlefield Events, and Louise Gomez of Manchester City Council for their efforts on our behalf.

With skillful selection of both new and commissioned work, John Gill has produced an exciting and thought-provoking show which explores the appeal of the game and how it is involved in the creation and reinforcement of national and individual identities and anxieties. We are grateful to him for his commitment to the project and to al

FOREWORD

he participating artists for kindly agreeing to
end existing works and for devoting considerable time and effort to making new ones. Our
thanks also to Simon Kuper and Richard Williams
for their excellent contributions and to all the
staff of Manchester City Art Galleries and the
nstitute of International Visual Arts who have
assisted in the preparation of this exhibition.

Richard Gray
Director
Manchester City Art Galleries

Gilane Tawadros
Director
Institute of International Visual Arts

INTRODUCTION

During the 1950s the Arts Council mounted football exhibition which comprised figurativ paintings by many leading twentieth centur artists of matches in progress and portraits c celebrated players. *Offside!* presents a markedl different aspect of the same national obsessior Though football continues as a source of idea and imagery for contemporary artists, few nov choose to approach the subject in such a direc and unquestioning way. It is not simply tha they seek to problemmatize their experience o football, but that they are aware of the multi plicity of debates which underscore the game and that current visual arts practice frees then to approach the subject in new, inventive ane perhaps more challenging ways.

This exhibition comprises newly commissionee and recent work by thirteen artists from Argentina, Britain, Colombia and Mexico. The selection procedure included an advertisec opportunity for artists to enter proposals for new commissions. Though several artists enjoyinc international reputations presented an obvious and valuable source of exhibition material, both curator and organisers were concerned to access other artists who were interested in working with the show's ideas and who might not have

OFFSIDE!

Contemporary Artists and
Football

John Gill

Lucy Gunning Video still from *The Footballers*

exhibited widely. The open submission enjoyed a popular and enthusiastic response and several of the proposals which were received have been realised for the exhibition. Using photography, video, painting and installation the exhibiting artists reference the imagery and text of football to explore the cultural environment of the game; the works identify the football stadium as an arena for the public display of national aspirations and anxieties, and the players as focuses of individual and national fantasy.

Roderick Buchanan's *Work in Progress*, previously shown at Tramway and the Lisson Gallery, is a display of 39 laminated photo-portraits taken in Glasgow, his home city, during 1993 and 1994. Visiting local five-a-side football pitches in a van with a portable, make-shift studio, Buchanan photographed players wearing Milanese shirts. At this exhibition he will field Glaswegian teams in the blue and black, and red and black of A C Milan and Inter Milan. In its effect on the visitor, this is probably the most immediately arresting and confusing work in the show; confronted with the familiar - players posed for publicity shots and presented together as a team - the spectator is at ease with the installation until the realisation that these are not Italian men. What city or nation do they represent if not Milan? After searching the physiognomy of the group for clues, for national characteristics etched in bone, and failing, we scrutinise the shirt and realise that apparel is only a fleeting indicator of preference and loyalty, to be worn with pride and to be discarded in a moment. We are reminded of this by Nick Waplington who has created four large-scale photographs based on team portraits available to the mass market as collectable stickers. The subjects of *Best of*

British are foreign nationals in British teams. The photographic process used here corrupts and remakes the image, and offers multiple choice for the representation of the team player. In a sporting culture which facilitates the purchase of city clubs by other cities, as in States' basketball and where players move between clubs nationally and internationally, these two sets of photographs are a portentous reminder of the transience and ambivalence of loyalties.

For Buchanan's new work, *Ten in a Million*, the seventh short video in a series which has included Budapest, Nantes, Glasgow, Berlin, New York and Amsterdam, he filmed the environment of 10 amateur pitches in Manchester from the central circle with a video camera on a slow revolve. Shown together the works are hypnotic and compelling; the silent, empty pitches at the heart of parkland or wasteland, housing or industrial estates, demolition and building sites are impassively recorded under leaden skies or bright sunlight. Martin Vincent and David Mackintosh present a contrasting view of game sites, more particularly stadia, which dominate their environments by physical scale and by the roar of the crowd. During March, the collaborative artists, who recently worked on *Video Positive* 1995, made a brief but hectic visit to Germany to film each of the German first division stadia. *Bundesliga (One World Cup and Two World Wars...)* is a newly commissioned video made by hand-held camera from a moving car. The artists keep up a dialogue during the filming, discussing the team they are visiting, German football, English and German culture, and much else. *Bundesliga* visits the sites of cultural exchange; because of Bayern and United, the distance between Munich and Manchester is les han European geography indicates.

n an attempt to realise the British conceit that var is simply another game, Crispin Jones presents a simple photograph of one of the footballs

That seemed to be the signal to attack' (Pte. L S Price quoted in M Middlebrook *The First Day on the Somme*, New York 1972). Jones has photographed Captain Nevill's football which is now in the collection of The Queen's Royal Surrey

Roddy Buchanan *Work in Progress* 1993-4. Installation at Tramway, Glasgow 1995   Photograph: the artist

which Capt. W P Nevill used at the Battle of the Somme, and provides a brief eyewitness account. Nevill bought four footballs, one for each of his platoons, and offered a prize to the first platoon to kick its ball up to the German trenches during the first wave of the assault near Montaubon: 'As the gun-fire died away I saw an infantry man climb onto the parapet into no-man's-land, beckoning others to follow. As he did so he kicked off a football; a good kick, the ball rose and travelled well towards the German lines.

Regimental Museum, Guildford, and reproduced large scale it achieves an iconic power.

Ultras, the installation of 66 canvasses by Adam Beebee, represents the banners of Italian football fans. Like other artists in the exhibition Beebee is an ardent football supporter and was drawn to Italian fans as the most 'passionate, frenzied and colourful'. Italian football clubs have up to five fan groups called *Ultras* ('utmost'); each group has its own name, often chosen to signify

Freddy Contreras
Stud 1996
shoes fitted with studs

Photograph: Stephen White

Freddy Contreras
Stud 1996
shoes fitted with studs

Photograph: Stephen White

Gabriel Kuri
Untitled 1996
printed adhesive labels and found objects

Photograph:the artist

Gabriel Kuri
Untitled 1996
printed adhesive labels and found objects

Photograph:the artist

From Nick Waplington
Best of British 1996
c-type colour photograph

Photograph:the artist

From Nick Waplington
Best of British 1996
c-type colour photograph

Photograph:the artist

strength and danger, such as *Hooligans*, *Skins*, *Furiosi* and *Bad Boys*. The groups are loosely federated, have a monthly magazine, *Supertifo*, and are usually twinned, different *Ultra* groups standing together at matches against the opposing team. Only the Juventus *Ultras* stand alone!

From Martin Vincent and David Mackintosh *Bundesliga (One World Cup and Two World Wars...)* 1996   photograph: the artists

In these circumstances the *Ultras'* colours acquire a strategic importance in the display of support and opposition. The work reproduces the flags or standards of the 66 dominant groups associated with Italy's 23 leading teams. The designs are based on team badges and team colours, and represent for example Juventus' *Vikings*, Lazio's *Eagles*, and Milan's *Commandos*. The canvasses were conceived as a single installation and are shown closely grouped and in the order the supported teams finished in the Italian League in the 1994-95 season.

This is the first occasion on which the Argentinian artist, Rosana Fuertes, has shown in Britain. She showed her vast installation *Pasió de multitudes*, imaginary football shirt designs on small, shaped boards, at the Havana Biennal in 1994. Though the work's monumentality impresses, it is the particularity of reference within each piece which preoccupies the observer. There are ironical political allusions, and also highly personal and tender homages to painters and friends. This 'codex of reminiscence', to use Gustavo Buntinx's description, moves across a range of decorative reference from heraldic to comic. Reproduced on the printed page, the shirts resemble mail-order advertisements for team strips, but your choice of purchase will not be a purely aesthetic decision. Fuertes presents a 'codex' of personal reference which you may buy into, but your preference will be informed by entirely individual preoccupations and separate cultural histories. The Glaswegian players in Buchanan's photographs choose to wear the shirts of Italian football clubs because of the associations vividly signified by the blue and red stripes and the team badges. A field of colour Fuertes' small shirts may appear merely decorative, and the regular template may harmonise the whole, but constituent parts insist on discovery and the observer is inevitably drawn into the search.

Lucy Gunning remade her video *The Footballers* at Manchester City Art Galleries in the space which accomodates *Offside!* shortly before the exhibition opened. The film, shown on a surveillance monitor outside the main exhibition space, hows two women kicking a football around the deserted gallery interior. In this, as in other videos by Gunning, women occupy spaces by participating in unfamiliar activities. They are wearing white coats, like doctors or medical attendants, and present a curious aspect to sanctuaries of national culture. Just as other works in the exhibition point to the pitch as a highly charged and defended space, occupied by the privileged few and observed by the many, so Gunning's short video precipitates a sense of outrage at the desecration of the gallery space

Video still from Roderick Buchanan *Ten in a Million* 1994-6 Glasgow

passers-by. Such illicit pleasures, presented as if accidentally for the scrutiny of gallery visitors, fascinate but are uneasily witnessed; similarly popular culture has, in the past, been excluded from positive relationships with 'high art'. For many the notion of football as a subject for fine art may be legitimised by the presence of respected artists in major public galleries, but for others the 'passion of the multitude' will never find appropriate expression in the protected

and of envy of these unknown women who have access and opportunity.

Gabriel Kuri has made commemorative pieces on previous occasions. He is fascinated by the emotional build up to major sports events and all the attendant hype. Kuri ironises the transience of the event in temporary structures which resemble market stalls. He collects discarded fruit boxes from the neighbourhood of the gallery and constructs stands which display phoney merchandise. The 'stock' is labelled with the imaginary logo of a future international football championship in place of the usual brand and country of origin. His last structure was laden with 80 coconuts, and Manchester's improvised stall includes locally available produce. With similar wit and considerable style the Colombian artist, Freddy Contreras, has assembled a collection of Vivienne Westwood shoes and has fitted each pair with a set of aluminium football studs. *Stud*, presents eleven pairs of identical, red, patent leather, three-strap stiletto-heeled shoes. Contreras' controversial and highly fetished new work, manipulates the relationships of sport and fashion, art and advertising, and the divisions of sexuality and gender.

Simon Patterson is represented by two pieces from 1990, *The Last Supper arranged according to the Flat Back Four Formation (Jesus Christ in Goal)*, and *The Last Supper arranged according to the Sweeper Formation (Jesus Christ in Goal)* which were first shown together at the Aperto of the 1993 Venice Biennale. The works, two rival teams, are painted directly onto the gallery walls. Patterson has used football as a metaphor in other works, notably *General Assembly* for the Chisenhale Gallery. The *Last Suppers*, inspired by the 1990 World Cup at Manchester, installed in opposition at the gallery entrance, immediately engage the visitor with the wit and subtlety of the artist's use of football imagery and text and invite many interpretations. Patricia Bickers points to 'the fundamentally different approaches to the game represented by the two teams drawn up against each other; the open game plan of the Europeans gives free play to Judas and St Peter; England's dogmatic adherence to

the flat back four formation condemns them t sit it out on the substitutes bench'.

Mark Wallinger, an artist who has regularly use football and racing in his work, uses many medi and varied approaches to the realisation of h ideas. Taking as a source of imagery the back page action photographs from newspaper Wallinger has used carbon paper to create series of 22 drawings which are a fastidiou reworking of captured moments from recen games. Using black and blue carbon paper t trace and identify each team player, he embarke upon a self-conscious regression to the obsessiv and adoring pleasure of his youth and has creat ed an installation which will find immediat appeal to many visitors who are similarly rapt.

Bet I Finish My Sticker Book Before You, a nev commission from Natalie Turner, also makes foray into the nostalgia of youth and sharec pleasures. She has recently been exploring football in a fine art context and is particularly interested in the ephemera and merchandising o football, and the marketing and status of the players. During past months she has been drawing the players and reserves selected for the European Football Championships. Her four-metre installation of over 300 tiny portraits, D-I-Y stickers drawn with felt tip pen on self-adhesive labels, is an obsessive tribute to the dedication of the fan, and contrasts the mass produced multiples of merchandising with the singular high-value icon of the drawn portrait.

Many of the works in the exhibition complement one another, working together with differing approaches technically and conceptually, and there are resonances between them which will pay a leisurely visit. Waplington's players enter into a tense dialogue with Buchanan's photos of local lads, and Fuertes' imaginary club strips take the field before Beebee's *Ultra* banners. Buchanan's quiet videos present a view from the centre of the amateur's deserted pitch, whilst the imposing architechture of the *Bundesliga* stadia in Vincent and Mackintosh's video diary both excites and excludes us. And Captain Nevill's football provides a disquieting punctuation in a visual narrative of subtle humour.

April 1996

'Maybe it's the same for Englishmen too', Luis Eduardo Soares, a Brazilian anthropologist, suggested to me. 'When Brazil plays, we feel that the identity of our country is being played out on the field. Our values are being shown to the world.'

Of course it is the same for Englishmen, and for almost everyone else too. The national football team, in a strange way, *is* the nation. People feel that the team's failings, its oddities, its strengths, tell them something about their country too.

Brazilians, for instance, have long debated how their team should play. ('I have a nation of football managers!', lamented one Brazilian coach, in an echo of Golda Meir.) The traditionalists, like João Saldanha, manager before the 1970 World Cup, argue that Brazil should play beautiful football and not worry too much about strategy. 'Brazilian football is a thing played to music', said Saldanha. Told that Pele, Gerson, Rivelino and Tostao could not possibly play in one midfield, he replied: 'I don't care if they are all the same type of player, or if Rivelino and Gerson are both left-footed. They are the best, they are geniuses, so let's trust them.'

The modernisers, men like Sebastiao Lazaroni,

manager at the 1990 World Cup, disagree. They use metaphors like 'machine' and say Brazil must be organised, more like the Germans. 'The national team must become less playful,' Lazaron warned, and he lived up to his word, fielding kind of Arsenal in canary shirts.

Brazil won the World Cup in 1994 under Carlo Alberto Parreira, who made a synthesis of both schools. But he was still too modern for mos Brazilians. Headed by the troika of Pele, Presiden Franco, and Parreira's mother, they complained that the team was too defensive.

These are not just arguments about football tactics; they are a debate about the kind of country Brazil should be. Should it be freewheeling and creative, and hang the rules, or should it try to become a kind of Germany? In 1990 Brazilians elected as president Fernando Collor de Mello, with a brief to "civilise" Brazil. Collor failed, becoming the most corrupt president the country could remember, but he was the political equivalent of the Lazaronis in football.

Football matters so much because the national team's matches are among the very few occasions when the nation is made flesh; when you

THE NATION MADE FLESH

by Simon Kuper

can actually *see* your country. The team is more alive than the flag, and more tangible than gross domestic product. The team *is* the nation. As the Mexican keeper Jorge Campos said at the last World Cup: 'Mexico attacks. That's what Mexico is.' For countries like Scotland that have no state, the team is even more important.

So when the team does badly, as England teams have in recent years, it makes people feel worse about their country. The mood in England is so low compared with ten years ago largely because the national symbols have been tarnished. The cricket and the football teams are doing badly; the Royal Family is a joke; John Major is quite a humble man, whereas Margaret Thatcher used to bang on endlessly about how marvellous the British were; and our economy is in decline. The Conservative Party wants to recreate the 'feel-good factor', but it is getting no help from our national teams. Harold Wilson understood how sport affected the public mood when he blamed his 1970 election defeat on England's elimination from the World Cup.

The England team affects the national mood not merely through its results. Debates over how the team should play, as in Brazil, mirror debates about what kind of a country we should be. Should we play old-fashioned, traditional, long-ball football, and hang the European way, or should we try to adapt to the Continental style? Under Graham Taylor, England did badly playing long-ball football. Many people subconsciously took this to suggest that anti-European Little England politics would make us a backward, unsuccessful nation.

And then there is money. England have sold their home matches to Sky Sport, so that only peopl with a satellite dish can see the team play, an have taken a sponsor, so that they are now offi cially The Green Flag England Team. For the larg swathe of the population that is more aware o soccer than politics - half the nation watche England lose to West Germany in 1990 - the T and sponsorship deals crystallise the feeling tha the people at the top of the country will do any thing for money. Selling the England team bring that home far more quickly than selling of British Gas. The team is the nation.

In new nations like Croatia, or nations seeking new identity like South Africa, sports teams ca help tell people what kind of a country they liv in. South Africa elected its first non-racial gov ernment in 1994. The next year the Springbok won the Rugby World Cup, and in 1996 the foot ball team won the African Nations Cup. Both victories were surprises, and made many Sout Africans feel that their nation had been blesse by God. His agent, of course, was Nelso Mandela - both the rugby and the football play ers said that they would have lost had he no spoken to them before certain matches. The vic tories also helped bring the races together, with Sowetans taking to the streets to celebrate the success of 14 Afrikaners and one black man in the Rugby World Cup.

Mandela constantly talked about the sports teams, using the football team, with its black, white and Coloured players, to suggest that the country's racial mix was a strength, not just a source of violence. Few clever politicians any-where ignore their football team. Mary Robinson, the Irish president, always defended Jack Charlton's right to pick players with only the aguest Irish links by saying that Ireland was not just its inhabitants but also its diaspora. Anyone with an Irish grandmother belonged. Not only did this nicely justify Ireland's footballing success, but also, the team was the diaspora made flesh. It said to people in Melbourne or New York or Glasgow: you are Irish too, and look how successful Ireland is! When Joseph O'Connor, in his book *The Secret World of the Irish Male*, imagined James Joyce being 'resuscitated, brought back to life, so he could play for the Republic of Ireland in the next World Cup', he was accepting that Joyce as a symbol was less important than Jack's Boys. No doubt David O'Leary's penalty against Rumania helped Mrs Robinson in her quest for diaspora investment, diaspora tourism, and diaspora support.

The Italian national team in 1994 was one of the few things in the country that was working. While leading politicians and businessmen were being arrested over bribery scandals, the national team was doing quite well and Silvio Berlusconi's AC Milan was the best side in the world. So Berlusconi founded a political party called Forza Italia - named after a football chant - and got himself elected prime minister, largely on the back of his work as president of Milan.

He had taken over the club in 1986, when it returned to Serie A after a 1979 bribery scandal, and then built an organised, rich team that beat allcomers from the rest of Europe. This was exactly what voters wanted him to do for the Italian state, stuck in the European second division after its own bribery scandal. He failed.

But football is not just a means of defining the nation. It can have a real, immediate effect on daily life. The most famous example is the Soccer War between Honduras and El Salvador in 1969. There were tensions between the two countries; then a series of football matches between them, with El Salvador qualifying for the World Cup on a disputed goal; and after that, the tanks rolled in. Football tells you something about your country, but also something about the country you play against. If it turns out that the people on the other side of the fence are cheating scum, then you have a duty to do something about this.

This is the way the Dutch saw their match against West Germany in the European Championships of 1988. To them, the two teams summed up the two countries. The Dutch players, wearing bright orange, played creative football, and most of them were fairly funny guys. Many were black. The Germans, by contrast, played dull football in black and white kit and all looked alike, while their fans made monkey noises at Holland's black players. To the Dutch, it seemed rather like the wartime German army all over again. So when Holland won 2-1, an estimated nine million people, most of the population, took to the streets on a Tuesday night to celebrate. The Rotterdam poet Jules Deelder, in a work called *21-6-88*, finished with these lines on Marco van Basten's winning goal:

Those who fell
Rose cheering from their graves.

'When Holland scores I dance through the room,' said Professor Dr L. De Jong, a small grey man who had spent 45 years writing the official history of the Netherlands in World War Two in umpteen volumes. 'I'm crazy about football,' he revealed. 'And what these boys have done! Of

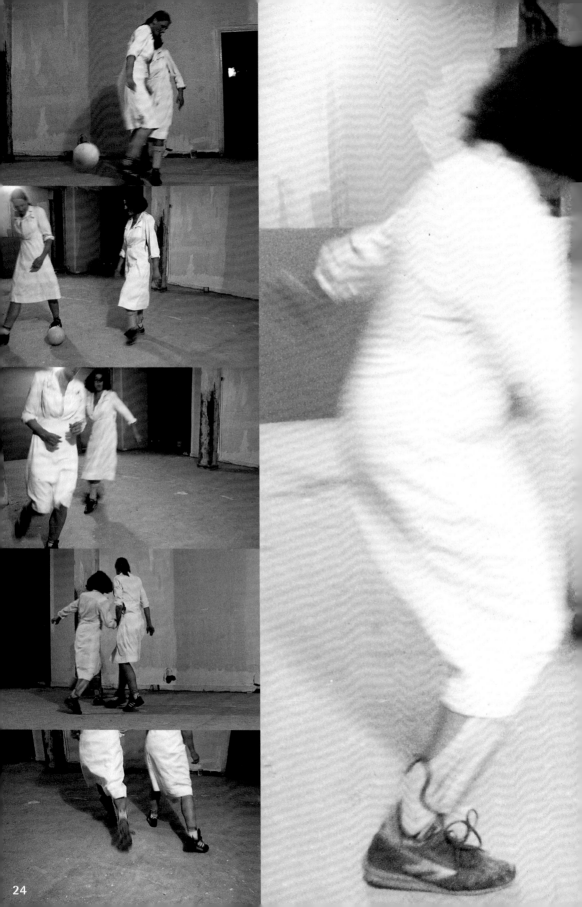

Video stills from
Lucy Gunning
The Footballers (1994 version)

Photographs: the artist

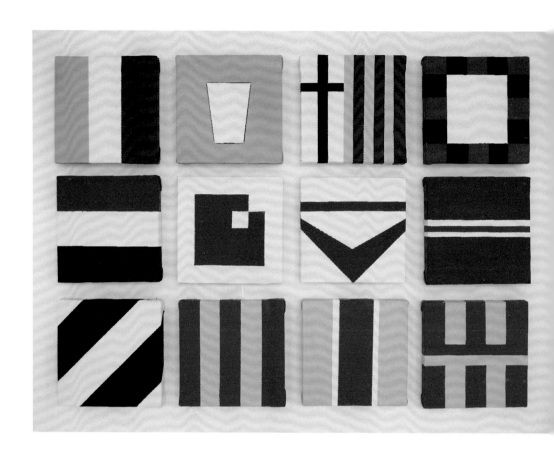

Adam Beebee
Ultras 1995 (detail)
acrylic on canvas

Photograph: University of Central Lancashire
Photography Department

Adam Beebee
Ultras 1995 (detail)
acrylic on canvas

Photograph: University of Central Lancashire
Photography Department

Crispin Jones
Captain Nevill 1996
mounted and laminated colour
photograph and text panel

Photograph: the artist

As the gun-fire died away I
saw an infantryman climb
onto the parapet and into No
Man's Land, beckoning
others to follow. As he did
so he kicked off a football;
a good kick, the ball rose
and travelled well towards
the German line. That
seemed to be the signal
to attack

Natalie Turner
Bet I Finish My Sticker Book Before You 1996
colour feltpen on self-adhesive labels

Photograph: the artist

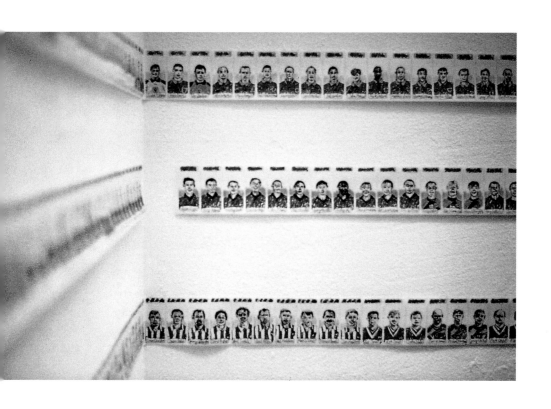

Natalie Turner
Premier League 1995
colour feltpen on self-adhesive labels
Installation 76 Marylebone High Street 1995

Photograph: the artist

from Mark Wallinger
vs. 1996
carbon on paper

Photographs: Peter White, FXP

from Mark Wallinger
vs. 1996
carbon on paper

Photograph: Peter White, FXP

ourse it's got to do with the War. Strange that people deny that.' As Rinus Michels, the Dutch manager in 1988, once, famously, said: 'Football war.'

ost Dutch people would have told you in 1988 nat they had hated the Germans since the War, not before. Maybe, but in the years before 988 their dislike had been fairly latent. ontemporary accounts of the Dutch-German World Cup final of 1974, for instance, show that ne match was played in a rather comradely spirit. ohn Rep and Paul Breitner, forbidden by FIFA om swapping shirts after the game, traded acket and tie at the post-match banquet. Ronald oeman and Olaf Thon swapped shirts in 1988, ut Koeman revealed on TV afterwards that he ad used Thon's shirt as toilet paper.

he reason that 1974 unleashed so little anti-German feeling is that the German team then vas quite creative and colourful and good itself. he football therefore offered no obvious Dutch-German contrasts. For most of the rest of the ost-war era, West Germany produced teams hat beat Holland.

o the match of 1988 was the first to offer an pparent morality play. Only football could dis-lay the differing characteristics of the two ountries - as the Dutch perceived them - so lainly. And so, from 1988, Dutch- German rela-ions began to worsen. Matches in 1990 and 992 caused skirmishes in border towns. German ars parked on Dutch streets would regularly have their windows broken or paintwork cratched. In an academic survey, Dutch eenagers named Germany as their least favourite country in the European Union. The

two governments panicked. Germany is Holland's leading trade partner by far, and the countries are close allies within the EU. Tensions began causing damage, with the involvement of the German firm DASA in the Dutch aeroplane com-pany Fokker prompting long debates in the Dutch parliament. So Helmut Kohl, the German chancellor, and Wim Kok, the Dutch prime min-ister acted. Kohl visited Rotterdam, whose town centre had been destroyed by German bombs, to lay a wreath, but he was jeered by a crowd of pensioners. He went to Amsterdam to watch Ajax play Bayern Munich, together with Kok, but the Dutch hammered Bayern in a bad-tempered game. And yet the tensions are healing, and the reason lies in football. The Dutch team is no longer so creative and good, the Germans are getting better, and so the morality play aspect of their encounters is disappearing.

Sometimes football is not conflict. World Cups and European Championships are carnivals of peoples, where fans from different countries meet, sing their folk songs, photograph each other and get drunk. The Dutch novelist Ronald Giphardt watched Holland beat Ireland in Orlando in 1994, and then hung out with the fans. He wrote: 'The main event of that evening: a Dutchman and an Irishman run into each other, look at each other, sag slightly at the knees and hug each other while screaming loudly.' And the fans tramped through Orlando, wearing each other's colours, and chanting, in unison: 'If you hate the fucking Germans clap your hands!'

'When you look at English football you ask, where is the George Best? Where are the skills?' The words of a Norwegian club manager whose team had just beaten the champions of England late in 1995 were spoken with a sort of sorrowful bewilderment. No doubt Nils Arne Eggen's Rosenborg met Blackburn Rovers on a particularly bad night, but his questions had been echoing around the football world long before the match of which he spoke.

For almost all of its history, the characteristics of English football have been passion and insularity. The passion was expressed in the emotional commitment of fans to clubs both great and small, and in the physical commitment of the players to a game based on strength and simplicity. It was turned into a constructive force in the World Cup victory of 1966, and during the long reign of British clubs in Europe between Manchester United's European Cup win in 1968 and the Heysel tragedy of 1985. Its reverse was the insularity which bred a disdain of foreigners based on the unacceptable contradiction of a natural assumption of superiority, endured during a long string of bitter defeats. For many years a related prejudice was turned inward, towards the black players who gradually and with extreme difficulty began to infuse the game with their character in the 1970s.

In some respects, nothing has changed. The attitude of the English team and their fans to their opponents and guests in the 1996 European Championship will tell us something about the evolution of attitudes surrounding the game. But in other areas the changes have been sudden and spectacular.

As I write this, on a Sunday evening in the early spring of 1996, I'm thinking about the two big football matches I've watched in London this weekend. The first, in the Premier League, featured a Romanian, a Dane, a citizen of the United States and a Dutchman who was once, although quite a long time ago, the world's greatest player. The second game, the final of the League Cup included a Serb, a Tobagan, a Ghanaian, a Swede, a South African and another US citizen. And of the 51 players (including substitutes) involved in the two games, no fewer than 17 were black. Elsewhere over the weekend, premier League matches were shaped by contributions from players with passports issued in France, Brazil, Iceland, Colombia, Germany, Holland, Nigeria, Georgia, Belgium, Russia and Switzerland. Only

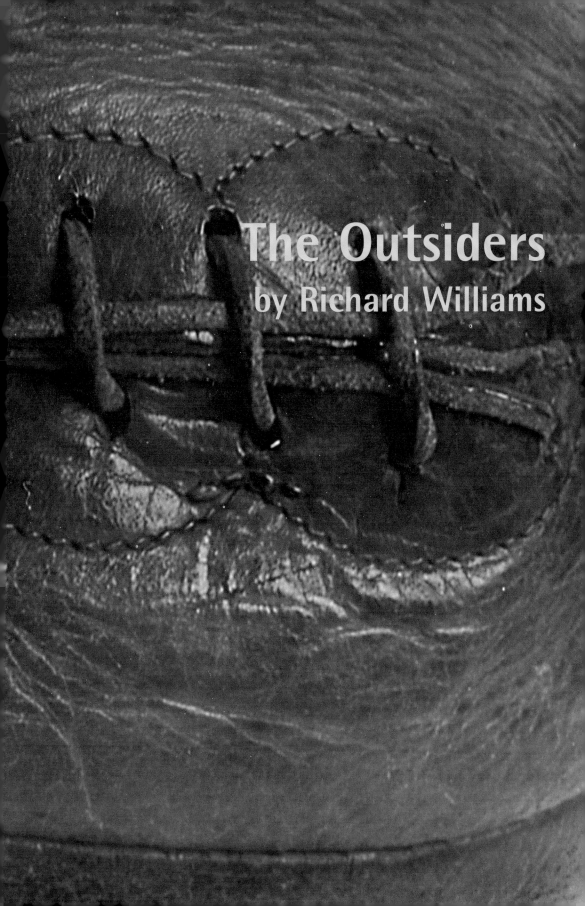

The Outsiders
by Richard Williams

one club, Liverpool, relied on a squad consisting solely of British players (although they included the son of a Jamaican soldier, one of three black players in the team). The course of the League Cup final at Wembley was set by an early goal from Aston Villa's Serb, Savo Milosevic, and concluded by a strike from his Tobagan partner, Dwight Yorke. An hour earlier, the result of the weekend's most significant match - and perhaps, by the time you read this, the destiny of the 1995-96 Premier League title - was determined by a goal from English football's most significant import, Eric Cantona of Manchester United and France.

When England won the World Cup in 1966, 'foreign' in terms of domestic football meant Scottish, Irish or Welsh. For many decades, those ethnic distinctions carried their own footballing values. The influx from Scotland carried a special significance. Almost. Every club had its resident Scot, sometimes a raw-boned centre half but more often a 'wee tanner ba' player', little men with fast feet who operated on the wings, twisting and turning to keep opposing full-backs busy. Today these skills are more likely to be imported from Sao Paulo or Tbilisi.

What we see now is an extraordinary transformation of a game long noted for its xenophobia into a kind of rainbow coalition which, at least in terms of variety, probably surpasses any ever assembled. The reasons for this are primarily driven by economics. After satellite TV started pouring money into the game at the beginning of 1995, the clubs could afford to match the wages offered in Italy or Spain, the traditional destinations of top players from less well endowed nations. Suddenly the ú20,000 a week

required by a Dennis Bergkamp or a Juninho became a realistic proposition. And these stars of the world game were needed in order to maintain the game's value at the box office, the qui pro quo for TV's investment and for the matching funds supplied by sponsors and equipment manufacturers. The other kind of variety was supplied by players of Afro-Caribbean origin but British nationality, whose tentative first steps in the game slowly became more confident, to the point that, at the beginning of 1996, the two most expensive home-produced players in the English game - Stan Collymore of Liverpool and Andy Cole of Manchester United - are both black.

In 1978 Viv Anderson, the Nottingham Forest full back, became the first black player to receive a full England cap, which was curious since the popular image of the black player was a silky winger with phenomenal speed but a supposedly uncertain heart for the winter game: the sort first glimpsed in the person of Albert Johanneson, the South African winger who played for Leeds United in the 1960s, and perpetuated in the likes of Laurie Cunningham, Vince Hilaire, Howard Gayle, Franz Carr and Ruel Fox. Eventually that stereotype was abandoned in the face of the emergence of midfielders like Paul Davis and Paul Ince, defenders like Paul Elliott and Des Walker (and, of course, the pioneering Anderson), goalkeepers like David James and Shaka Hislop, and powerful strikers like Cole and Collymore. Yet some significant judges, even those at the pinnacle of power in the English game, persisted in their prejudice - perhaps unconscious - against the black players.

But the true mondialisation of English football

really dates from the autumn of 1978, the year of Anderson's England debut, when Keith Burkinshaw, the doleful Yorkshireman who then managed Tottenham Hotspur, agreed to a deal already passed up by his greatest rival, Terry Neill of Arsenal, and brought the Argentinian players Osvaldo Ardiles and Ricardo Villa to north London. Both men were fresh from playing prominent roles in their country's World Cup triumph, a home victory for the military junta. Many British observers besides Terry Neill were sceptical of their ability to adapt to the exigencies of the British game. Once here, the tiny, light-footed Ardiles and the big, moustachioed Villa displayed contrasting styles but shared a common artistry which turned out to blend well with Spurs' traditional cultured approach, as embodied in their new midfield accomplice, the young Englishman Glenn Hoddle. The reward for Burkinshaw's faith came at the end of their third season in England, when Villa's solo dribble through the heart of the Manchester City penalty area gave his team victory in the FA Cup Final and bequeathed to the competition one of its most glorious individual moments. Villa went home at the end of that season, while the sudden eruption of conflict in the Falkland Islands persuaded Ardiles that he should pursue his calling elsewhere for a while. He shared his countrymen's belief that the Malvinas belonged to them, but when the war was over he returned to White Hart Lane and to a fond place in the hearts of all English football fans, who had quickly recognised his special combination of skill and courage. When injury forced Ardiles to retire in 1986, the kick-off of his farewell testimonial match - against Internazionale of Milan - had to be delayed for half an hour because of the crush of fans trying to get in. Diehard Tottenham fans, grateful for his contribution, mingled with neutrals merely wanting to express their thanks for the years of pleasure he had given them. The fact that Ardiles's friend Diego Maradona had travelled from Naples to make a guest appearance for the English team seemed incidental. Ardiles's later adventures as a manager - success at Swindon, failure at Newcastle, humiliation at Tottenham - did nothing to impair the affection in which he was held by the vast majority of the English football public.

Before Ardiles and Villa, foreigners had existed in the English game as anomalies. In the Fifties there were the powerful Robledo brothers, George and Ted, two of the three sons of a Chilean father and an English mother. When their parents split up, their mother brought the boys back home to Yorkshire, where they were schooled and eventually signed by Barnsley. George, a barnstorming centre forward, and Ted, a wing-half, went on to Newcastle United, where George's exploits alongside Jackie Milburn made him one of the legends of St. James' Park. George won an FA Cup winners' medal in 1951, when Milburn scored both goals against Blackpool; a year later, joined by Ted, George scored the only goal of the game against Arsenal as the Magpies made it two in a row. Later he returned to Chile, where he played for the Colo-Colo club and the national team. And then there were those who had 'stayed on' after the war: the former prisoners of war, such as Bert Eisentranger, a half-back with Bristol City, and Bert Trautmann, Manchester City's goalkeeper, who earned a place in posterity as well as a winners' medal after playing on heroically through the 1956 Cup Final with a broken neck.

Video stills from
Martin Vincent and David Mackintosh
Bundesliga (One World Cup and Two World Wars...) 1996

Photographs: the artists

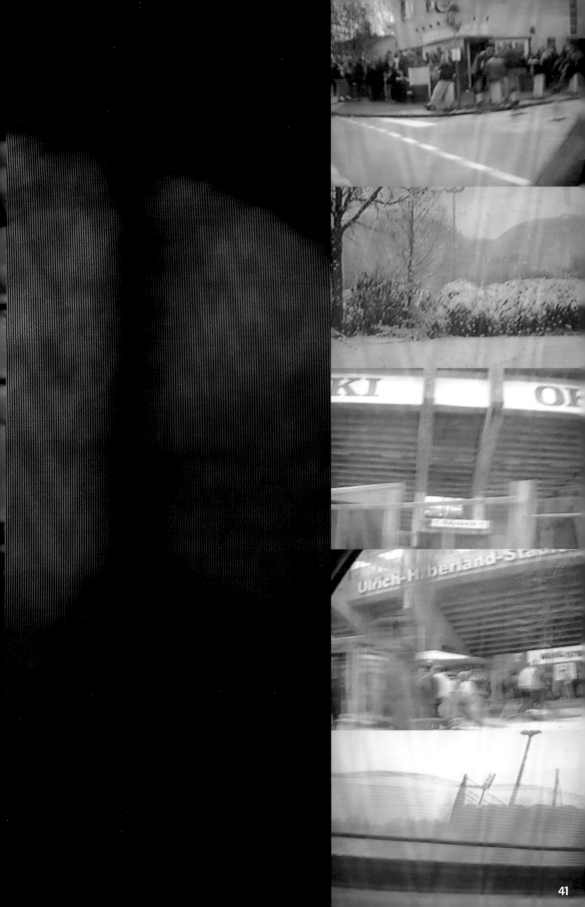

Players who associate themselves with Italian football by
wearing Inter Milan and A.C. Milan shirts amid the dozens
of local tops on display every night on the football parks
of Glasgow.
Photographs taken between September 1993 and
September 1994.

from Roderick Buchanan
Work in Progress 1993-94
39 mounted and laminated colour photographs

Photographs: the artist

Rosana Fuertes
Pasión de multitudes 1992-3 (detail)
acrylic on board

Photograph: the artist

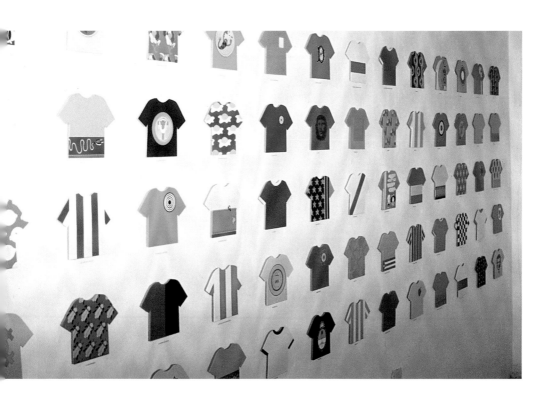

Rosana Fuertes
Pasión de multitudes 1992-3
Installation Havana Biennale 1994

Photograph: the artist

Christ

St. Philip   St. John   St. Thomas   St. Andrew

St. Bartholomew

St. Matthew   St. Simon

St. Thaddeus

St. James the Less   St. James the Greater

St. Peter

Judas

Simon Patterson
The Last Supper Arranged According to the Flat Back
Four Formation (Jesus Christ in Goal) 1990
acrylic paint on gallery wall

Christ

St.Peter

St.John   St.Philip

St. Thaddeus   St. Bartholomew

St. Andrew   Judas   St. Simon

St. Thomas   St. Matthew

St. James the Less

St. James the Greater

Simon Patterson
The Last Supper Arranged According to the Sweeper
Formation (Jesus Christ in Goal) 1990
acrylic paint on gallery wall

Video still from
Roderick Buchanan
Ten in a Million 1994-6
Glasgow

above left: municipal football pitch, Marseille
above right: municipal football pitch, Köln

Photographs: Simon Starling

The Forties and Fifties were a period of slow awakening for English football, of a gradual erosion of the assumption of superiority. Moscow Dynamo arrived in London immediately after the war and drew three-all with Chelsea in front of 100,000 at Stamford Bridge; then, in a dense fog, they beat Arsenal 4-3, even though the home team had borrowed a pair of star England forwards, Stanley Matthews and Stan Mortensen, to reinforce their own depleted forces. Eight years later the Hungarians came to Wembley and became the first side to beat England on their home ground - by the traumatising margin of 6-3. Ferenc Puskas's drag-back to beat Billy Wright, England's admirable captain, before scoring the third goal with a superb left-foot shot was a moment matched only twice for dramatic beauty in England's history of trauma: first by the dazzling move involving Roberto Rivelino, Tostao and Pele, and reaching a climax with Jairzinho's low shot, by which Brazil defeated England in the 1970 World Cup finals in Mexico, and 16 years later, in the same country, when Maradona went on his endless celebratory slalom through the defence which, four minutes earlier, he had mocked with his hand-ball goal. The Hungarians, just to prove something or other, won the return fixture in Budapest a few months later, this time by 7-1. And in 1957, having entered the competition in the teeth of the Football Association's xenophobic disapproval, Manchester United were beaten in the semi-final of the European Cup by Real Madrid, with Alfredo Di Stefano and Raymond Kopa prominent in the white shirts of the Spanish champions.

If the influx of foreign players has become a flood in recent years, the outflow has never been more than a trickle. In the early Fifties, a handful of players briefly responded to overtures from Colombian clubs, who offered salaries that trebled and quadrupled the iniquitous 'maximum wage' of the English game. Soon British players were receiving approaches from the rich Italian clubs, although few prospered. Jimmy Greaves, Joe Baker and Denis Law came back telling tales of mismatched cultural experiences. But John Charles, the giant Welshman equally at ease leading the attack or at the centre of the defence, became one of the best loved players ever to pull on the Juventus shirt in Turin. Not much was destined to change: several generations later, it was possible to delete the names of Greaves, Baker and Law and insert those of Ian Rush, Luther Blissett, Des Walker and Paul Gascoigne, all of whom returned richer in material things but diminished as players. Even David Platt, whose various transfers between a series of Italian clubs set a world record for aggregate fees for a single player, made little lasting impression. Mark Hughes, after spells with Barcelona and Bayern Munich, had to return to Manchester United to rehabilitate his career. Ray Wilkins, Trevor Francis, Joe Jordan and Liam Brady achieved more, as did Glenn Hoddle in Monaco and Gary Lineker with Barcelona, but in 1995-96 only Paul Ince at Internazionale in Milan and Tony Cascarino at Olympique Marseille represented the British leagues in the Mediterranean countries.

The traffic was coming the other way. If Bert Trautmann had played his part in giving former German combatants a new image, Ardiles and Villa 20 years later provided the conclusive proof that alien talent, even in its most Latinate incarnations, would not necessarily fade and perish in the chill of an English winter. After them, the

ates opened. At Manchester United, Dave Sexton brought Nicky Jovanovic, a centre-back, from Red Star Belgrade; he was followed to Old Trafford by Jesper Olsen, the nimble Danish winger. Bobby Robson transformed bucolic Ipswich Town in the Seventies through the skills of two Dutchmen, Arnold Muhren and Frans Thijssen, the former later transferring his calm vision to Manchester United with similar success. The Polish schemer Kazimierz Deyna, a member of the team that had denied England qualification to the 1974 World Cup finals, joined Manchester City. Johnny Metgod, a balding Dutchman, brought his precise deliberations and powerful shooting from Real Madrid to Nottingham Forest. Jan Molby, a tubby Dane, left Ajax to pull the strings in the Liverpool midfield. Nico Claessen, a deft Belgian goalpoacher, stayed for a while at White Hart Lane.

Others fared less well, and the supporters of most major clubs have dim memories of a lacklustre Yugoslav or two on the substitutes' bench at some time in the Eighties. Some imports left a clearer after-image without doing much to lift the fortunes of their clubs. A third member of the Argentinian World Cup-winning team, the heavily permed right back Alberto Tarantini, could not settle in Birmingham, either to the football or the culture (in the early weeks of 1996, back home in Argentina, he was arrested and charged with possession of cocaine and ecstasy). Further failures included Raimondo Ponte, a little Swiss midfielder, at Forest; Mirandinha, the first Brazilian, at Newcastle, where his only lasting legacy might be said to be the introduction of Lycra cycling shorts to the match-day kit of the English league professional; the bafflingly unproductive Nikki Petrovic at

Arsenal; Romeo Zondervan, a third Dutchman at Ipswich, who made far less impact than Muhren or Thijssen; Alex Sabella, an Argentinian prodigy whose gifts failed to bloom at Sheffield United; and the winger Didier Six at Aston Villa, the first Frenchman of any consequence in the English game, but hardly a good advertisement despite his appearances in the great national team of the Michel Platini years.

Most bizarre of all, for a season it was possible to make the journey down to the dilapidated canyons of the Valley in South London to see the Danish forward Allan Simonsen, the European player of the year, performing his delicate tricks to the vast unpopulated terraces in tandem with Derek Hales, a Londoner with a piratical beard and an uncompromising attitude to opposing defenders. Seldom can two forwards have been juxtaposed to such hilarious effect; unsurprisingly, Simonsen was soon on his travels again, and the fans of Charlton Athletic were left rubbing their eyes and wondering what kind of a dream they had just awoken from.

The modern era could be said to have begun when Eric Cantona chose England as the location for the rebirth of his wrecked career in January 1992. Signed for úl million by Howard Wilkinson, Leeds United's manager, Cantona found other French-speakers at Elland Road - Lee Chapman, who had played briefly at Niort, and two younger men, Kevin Sharp and Jamie Forrester, who had taken the enterprising step of apprenticing themselves to Guy Roux's Auxerre before returning to English football - but throughout his stay in Leeds he was noted for his reticence.

Cantona lasted only half a season at Leeds before

falling out with Wilkinson, who recouped his money by selling the player on to Manchester United in what quickly proved to be the bargain of the footballing century. The results were to speak for themselves: three championships and an FA Cup winner's medal in his first three seasons in England. And if that were not evidence enough, his new manager, Alex Ferguson, spoke with bubbling enthusiasm about 'mon genius'. No one, least of all Ferguson, doubted that Cantona had been the catalyst (the manager's own word) of the team's first championship in 26 years. Where there had been anxiety, Cantona instilled confidence. He alone played as if Manchester United's short-term destiny were not a problem that would be solved by fretting. Whatever reservations may have lingered in some quarters, even after the Ardiles-Villa and Thijssen-Muhren contributions, about the ability of foreigners to flourish and wield influence within the English game, the Frenchman demolished them for all time. And during the course of 1995, when between January and November he underwent the extraordinary chain of events that followed his kung-fu kick at a neo-Nazi fan after being sent off against Crystal Palace, he wrote one of the most amazing chapters in the history of the English game, returning after an eight-month suspension to provide a demonstration that he had grown up enough to control his volatile nature, even though his very personal sense of right and wrong was probably unaffected.

The Cantona effect was felt everywhere. Now club managers realised what benefits could be achieved through the addition of foreign players, with their technical skill and tactical originality, not to mention their superior levels of fitness and preparation, and their understanding of dietary requirements. The most thoroughl mindboggling example of the change arrive one grey weekday morning in November 199 when several thousand people turned up a Middlesbrough's brand new ground, th Riverside Stadium, built on reclaimed with money from the Football Trust, Sky TV and a enthusiastic young chairman. They were takin the morning off from schools and jobs to wel come the arrival of another investment, th Brazilian playmaker Oswaldo Giraldo Junior, better known as 'Juninho', brought to their club by Bryan Robson, now Middlesbrough's manage but once the most E:nglish of players, for a fee o ú4.5 million. There were fans in Brazilian national shirts with Juninho's name on the back, i sombreros, carrying banners welcoming the player in his native Portuguese language. There wa an ad hoc samba band from the local college o education, doing their best to make the new arrival feel at home. And within days they ha the pleasure of the tiny, impossibly deft Brazilian bring yet another new dimension to the natior that invented the game.

'There's no argument from me about the good things that the foreigners have brought to our game,' the thoughtful veteran coach Dave Sexton said the following day, when I talked to him about the arrival of Juninho. 'Some of them have trouble adapting to our system of play. But Cantona is probably the best example of the benefits that are there to be had. Obviously the young players at Old Trafford have learnt an awful lot from him. But some of the older players have been influenced by him, too. They wouldn't have played that way if he'd never been there.'

And after Cantona there came Jurgen Klinsmann, a millionaire who drove an old Beetle and was named player of the year for his single season of euphoric goalscoring with Tottenham ('But he's got a Porsche in the garage,' said his team mate Darren Anderton, hinting at the German's command of public relations skills); the great Ruud Gullit, playing an influential twilight season at Chelsea; Philippe Albert, David Ginola and Faustino Asprilla, the high-definition performers in Newcastle United's championship bid; and Juninho and Curcic and Dani and Kinkladze and Roy and Bergkamp and scores more, including a trio of Spaniards at Wigan Athletic, known to the fans as the Three Amigos, and an Italian at Grimsby who got involved in a well publicised punch-up with his manager. Some of them (like Cantona, the most notable) have been exiles and misfits, cast out of their own lands, a legion of the misunderstood, but they are all members of a procession which, although it may not have raised the quality of English football to the very highest level, has nevertheless made the game an infinitely more entertaining and artistically satisfying proposition.

In the process, all sorts of consciousnesses have been raised. The final word might best be given to Graham Kelly, chief executive of the Football Association, a notoriously glum figure who symbolises to many the inability of English football to amend and update its fundamental values. Kelly invariably looks like a man whose team has just been eliminated in the third round of the FA Cup by a bunch of part-timers. Yet he is a sincere and erudite lover of the game, brave enough to have envisioned handing over the job of reshaping the structure of English football to a Frenchman. Ask him about the foreign players, and you get a little speech that approaches the condition of poetry, a masterpiece of ecstatic compression, a sort of terrace haiku: 'Cantona - a thing of beauty. His flicks, his feints, the way he takes the ball on the outside of his instep - I could watch him all day. Klinsmann won everyone over. Bergkamp, Ginola, Juninho - they can only be an influence for good.'

EXHIBITING ARTISTS

ADAM BEEBEE born Wolverhampton **1973**. Studied **1992–1993** at Stourbridge Art College on the Foundation Course, and **1993–1996** at the University of Central Lancashire for BA(Hons) Fine Art.

EXHIBITIONS: 1995 *UCL Group Show* Harris Museum & Art Gallery, Preston **1996** *Degree Show* University of Central Lancashire

RODERICK BUCHANAN born Glasgow **1965**. Studied **1984–1989** Glasgow School of Art for BA, and **1989–1990** University of Ulster, Belfast.

SELECTED EXHIBITIONS: 1989 *The Festival of Plagiarism*, Transmission Gallery, Glasgow; *Information*, Paisley Museum & Art Gallery **1990** *The Recky*, North Queen Street Community Centre Belfast; *Self Conscious State*, Third Eye Centre Glasgow **1991** *The Living Room*, a Gianni Piacentini project, Army Orpheus Gallery, Belfast; *Speed*, Transmission Gallery, Glasgow; *Windfall*, Glasgow **1992** *Contact*, Transmission Gallery, Glasgow; *Outing Art*, BBC Billboard Project; *Guilt by Association*, Irish Museum of Modern Art, Dublin **1993** *International Departures*, Die Gesellschaft für Aktuelle Kunst, Bremen; *Coalition*, Centre for Contemporary Arts, Glasgow; *Wonderful Life*, Lisson Gallery, London; *Roderick Buchanan*, Knoll Gallery, Vienna **1994** Oriel Mostyn, Llandudno; *Scottish Video*, Museum of Installation, London; *Institute of Cultural Anxiety*, ICA, London **1995** *Ideal Standard*

Summertime, Lisson Gallery, London; *Karaoke*, outh London Art Gallery; City Racing, London; Glasgow Print Studios **1996** *Looking Awry*, Brazilian Embassy, Paris.

FREDDY CONTRERAS born Bogota, Colombia 1956. Studied **1984-1987** Chelsea School of Art for BA(Hons) Fine Art, **1987-1989** Royal College of Art for MA Fine Art/Sculpture, and 1990-1991 Kings College, University of London, Spanish American Studies (Literature and Anthropology).
SELECTED EXHIBITIONS: 1987 *Four Schools of Thought*, James Hockey Gallery, Farnham; *Top Marks*, London Institute Gallery **1988** *London Art Schools in Belgium*, Ecole en Gallerie, Brussels **1989** *MurMur*, The Crypt Gallery, London; *Concept 88 Reality 89*, University Gallery, Colchester **1990** *Claensian*, The Vaughan Music Room and Somerville College, Oxford; South London Art Gallery, London **1991** Gimpel Fils, London **1992** *Fin de Semena*, Mario Flecha Gallery, London; *Hit and Run*, Tufton Street, London **1993** *Good Work*, Bonington Gallery, Nottingham University; *Three Installations*, 194 Goldhawk Road, London **1994** *Installations*, Small Mansions Arts Centre, London **1995** The Showroom, London.

ROSANA FUERTES born Mar del Plata, Argentina **1962**. Studied Escuela Superior de Artes Visuales Martin Malharro, Mar del Plata.
INDIVIDUAL EXHIBITIONS: 1992 *Peoples*

Passion, Giesso Gallery, Buenos Aires; *Paintings*, Casal de Catalunya, Buenos Aires **1993** Institute of Cooperation Iberoamericano, Buenos Aires **1994** *Installation*, White Columns, New York **1995** *Paintings*, Camargo Vilaca Gallery, Sao Paulo.
GROUP EXHIBITIONS: 1991 *Nexus*, Giesso Gallery, Buenos Aires **1992** *4 + 2*, Sara Garcia Uriburu Gallery, Buenos Aires; *New World Foundation to the New Painting*, National Museum of Fine Arts, Buenos Aires **1993** *Tele-Aesthetics*, Protect Art Center, New York; *Utilisima*, Palais de Glace, Buenos Aires; *Erotic Art*, Recoleta Cultural Center, Buenos Aires **1994** *Southern Wind*, Cultural Center G Mayer, Brasilia and tour; *Update Show*, White Columns, New York; *Quinta Bienal de La Habana*, Museum of Fine Art, Havana; *ARCO*, Jacob Karpio Gallery, Miami **1995** *Perverse Childhood*, Museum of Modern Art, Rio de Janeiro; *Artists' Books*, Wilfredo Lam Center, Havana **1996** *Juego de Pelota*, Borges Cultural Centre, Buenos Aires.

LUCY GUNNING born Newcastle Upon Tyne **1964**. Studied **1983-1984** West Surrey College of Art & Design for Diploma in Foundation Studies, **1984-1987** Falmouth School of Art, Cornwall for BA(Hons) Fine Art, and **1992-1994** Goldsmiths' College, University of London for MA Fine Art.
SELECTED EXHIBITIONS: 1987 *Whitworth Young Contemporaries*, Whitworth Gallery,

Manchester **1988** *Group Installation,* Green Room, Manchester **1989** *Site Specific Sculpture,* Berllanderi Sculpture Workshop, Gwent/ **1991** *Out of Context,* Hallam Fine Art, London; *Collaborative Installation,* Open Space Gallery, Reading **1993** *Super 8 Moments,* London Film Makers Co-op **1994** Nikolai Wallner Gallery, Copenhagen; Cologne Art Fair, Cologne; *The Ecstasy of Limits,* Gallery 400, Chicago; *Wish You Were Here,* London & Newcastle; *Out of the Nineties,* Mall Galleries, London; *The Curator's Egg,* Anthony Reynolds Gallery, London; *BT New Contemporaries,* London and tour **1995** *Kine (Kunst) 95,* Belgium; *Video Positive,* Liverpool; *Lucy Gunning,* Adam Gallery, London.

CRISPIN JONES born London **1974.** Studied **1993–1996** Kingston University for BA(Hons) Fine Art (Sculpture).
EXHIBITIONS: 1994 *Abducted,* London Film Makers Co-op; *Make Believe,* South Bank Photo Show 94, London; Kaliski Open **1995** *Outpost,* Venice Biennale; **2,* Kingston Sorting Office.

GABRIEL KURI born Mexico City **1970.** Studied **1988–1992** Escuela Nacional de Artes Plasticas, Universidad Nacional Autonoma de Mexico for BA Visual Arts, and **1993–1995** Goldsmiths' College, University of London for MA Fine Art. **1987–1991** Gabriel Orozco's workshop.
SELECTED EXHIBITIONS: 1989 *Novos Valores da Arte Latino Americana e Internacional,* Brasilia Museum of Art, Brazil **1990** *Aire Fresco en el Verano del Amor,* Galeria Division Arte, Mexico D F **1991** *D F Art from Mexico City,* Blue Star Art Space, San Antonio; *Reconsideracion del Paisaje 10 Installations,* Club Hipico La Sierra, Mexico D F, Iconografia del Capricho Galeria Etnia, Mexico D F **1992** *Cuerpo Compartido,* Foro Cultural Roxy, Guadalajara, Mexico D F; *Te Amo Pero Donde Estas,* Galeria Arte Actual Mexicano, Monterrey, Mexico D F **1993** *Otros Especimenes,* Museo Universitario del Chopo, Mexico D F; Calma Temistocles 44, Mexico D F **1994** *Kunst Fair,* Nicolai Wallner Gallery, Cologne; *Private View,* Chisenhale Gallery, London; *The Return of Cadavre Exquis,* The Drawing Center, New York **1995** Nicolai Wallner Gallery, Copenhagen; *MA Degree Show,* Goldsmiths' College, London **1996** *Everyday Holiday,* Le Magasin Centre d'Art Contemporain, Grenoble.

DAVID MACKINTOSH born Sunderland **1966.** Studied **1984–1985** and **1986–1989** Sunderland Polytechnic for BA(Hons) Fine Art.
SELECTED EXHIBITIONS: 1993 *Random Fictions* (with Martin Vincent), Manchester Boardwalk **1994** *Diverse City,* Castlefield Gallery, Manchester **1995** *Wow + Flutter,* Chapman Gallery, Salford; *Jolly Peril Paradise,* Castlefield Gallery, Manchester; *Recent Paintings,* Aytoun Gallery, Manchester; *Hearing is Believing* (with Martin Vincent), Video

Positive 95, Liverpool; *Ha!*, 10a Little Peter Street, Manchester.

SIMON PATTERSON born Leatherhead **1967.** Studied **1985-1986** Hertforshire College of Art & Design Foundation Course, and **1986-1989** Goldsmiths' College, University of London for BA(Hons) Fine Art.
INDIVIDUAL EXHIBITIONS: 1989 Third Eye Centre **1991** Riverside Studios, London **1993** The Grey Art Gallery, New York **1994** *General Assembly*, Chisenhale Gallery, London; *Simon Patterson: The Chamber of the House of Lords/ Herbacious Border Plants (Hardy Perennials)*, Kluuvi Gallery, Helsinki **1995** Gandy Gallery, Prague; Kohji Ogura Gallery, Nagoya; Rontgen Gallery, Tokyo **1996** Lisson Gallery, London.
GROUP EXHIBITIONS: 1988 *Freeze Parts 1 & 3*, London Docklands **1989** *1789-1989: Ideas and Images of Revolution*, Kettle's Yard, Cambridge **1990** *Group Show Parts 2 & 4*, Milch Gallery, London **1991** *New Work*, Transmission Gallery, Glasgow **1992** *A Modest Proposal*, Milch Gallery, London; *Instructions and Diagrams*, Victoria Miro Gallery, London; *Etats Spécifiques*, Musée des Beaux-arts André Malraux, Le Havre; *Contact*, Transmission Gallery, Glasgow; *In and Out and Back and Forth*, 578 Broadway, New York; *With Attitude*, Galerie Rodolphe Janssen, Brussels; *Instructions Received*, Gio' Marconi, Milan; *Doubletake*, Hayward Gallery, London **1993** *Il Mistero dei 100 Dollari Scomparsi*, Studio Marconi, Milan;

Aperto, Venice Biennale; *Wonderful Life*, Lisson Gallery, London **1994** *High Fidelity*, Kohji Ogura Gallery, Nagoya; *Surface de Réparations*, FRAC Bourgogne, Dijon; *Wall to Wall*, Southampton City Art Gallery; *Art et la Megapole*, Galerie Philippe Huzzan, Paris; *Five British Artists*, Andrehn Schiptjenko, Stockholm; *Mapping*, Museum of Modern Art, New York; *Fiction - Non Fiction*, Galleria Alessandra Bonomo, Rome; *The Curator's Egg*, Anthony Reynolds Gallery, London; *Seeing the Unseen*, Invisible Museum, London; *Esprit d'Amusement*, Grazer Kunstverein, Graz; *The Institute of Cultural Anxiety - Works from the Collection*, ICA, London **1995** ArtAngel Project, *Ideal Standard Summertime*, Lisson Gallery, London.

NATALIE TURNER born Birkenhead **1966.** Studied **1986-1989** Camberwell School of Art for BA(Hons) Fine Art.
SELECTED EXHIBITIONS: 1986 Williamson Art Gallery, Birkenhead **1989** *SOGAT Show*, South London Art Gallery **1992** Bridewell Gallery, Liverpool, 63 Union Street, London **1993** *Pet Show*, 63 Union Street, London **1994** *Tinsel*, Adam Gallery, London; *Some Paintings*, Adam Gallery, London **1995** *Hardwork-Shift Two*, 43 Exmouth Market, London; *Mary the Bone*, 76 Marylebone High Street, London **1996** *Habitat*, Finchley Road, London.

MARTIN VINCENT born Stoke-on-Trent **1962.** Studied **1980-1981** North Staffordshire

Polytechnic, and **1981–1984** Manchester Polytechnic for BA(Hons) Fine Art.

SELECTED EXHIBITIONS: 1992 *Work and Play,* Castlefield Gallery, Manchester; *Jamie Collins - Martin Vincent - Vivienne Ware,* Manchester City Art Galleries; *Random Fictions* (with David Mackintosh), Manchester Boardwalk; *Monsters from Seven Continents* (with Mike Noon), Manchester Festival **1993** *Go Gojira,* Keele University Gallery **1994** *The Big Picture,* (with Basement Video Project) Cornerhouse, Manchester **1995** *Hearing is Believing* (with David Mackintosh), Video Positive 95, Liverpool; *Someone to Comfort Me,* Widnes Railway Station; Roadhouse, Manchester; *Ha!,* 10a Little Peter Streeet, Manchester.

MARK WALLINGER born Chigwell **1959.** Studied **1977–1978** Loughton College, **1978–1981** Chelsea School of Art, and **1983–85** Goldsmiths' College, London for MA.

INDIVIDUAL EXHIBITIONS: 1988 *Passport Control,* Riverside Studios, London; Burgess Park Nottingham Castle Museum **1990** *School,* Sophia Ungers, Cologne; *Stranger 2,* Anthony Reynolds Gallery, London **1991** *Capital,* Grey Art Gallery, New York and tour **1992** *Fountain,* Anthony Reynolds Gallery, London **1993** Daniel Newburg Gallery, New York **1994** *The Full English,* Anthony Reynolds Gallery, London **1995** Ikon Gallery, Birmingham, Serpentine Gallery, London**1996** Deweer Art Gallery, Otegem.

RECENT GROUP EXHIBITIONS: 1989 *Territories* Chisenhale Gallery, London; *Excommunication; Some Notions of Marginality* Grey Art Gallery, New York **1990** The Koln Show Cologne **1991** *Confrontaciones,* Palacio de Velasquez, Madrid **1992** *Whitechapel Open,* Clove Building, London; *Let Me Look,* San Miniato **1993** *Young British Artists II,* Saatchi Collection, London; *Spit in the Ocean,* Anthony Reynolds Gallery, London; *You've Tried the Rest, Now Try The Best,* City Racing, London; *Mandy Loves Declan 100%,* Mark Boote Gallery, New York **1994** *Jet Lag,* Galerie Martina Detterer, Frankfurt; *Every Now and Then,* Rear Window, London; *Not a Self Portrait,* Karsten Schubert Gallery, London; *Here and Now,* Serpentine Gallery, London; *Untitled Streamer Eddy Monkey Full Stop Etcetera,* Anthony Reynolds Gallery, London; *Seeing the Unseen,* Thirty Shepherdess Walk, London; *Art Unlimited,* National Touring Exhibition **1995** *The Art Casino,* Barbican Art Gallery, London; *John Moores Exhibition 19,* Liverpool; *The British Art Show,* Manchester and tour; *The Turner Prize,* Tate Gallery, London.

NICK WAPLINGTON born Scunthorpe **1965.** Studied Trent Polytechnic, and Royal College of Art.

INDIVIDUAL EXHIBITIONS: 1990 *Family Pictures,* Pomeroy Purdy Gallery, London; *Living Room,* The Photographers' Gallery, London and tour **1992** *Living Room & Circles of Civilisation,*

hiladelphia Museum of Art; *The Isaac Mizrahi Pictures,* James Danziger Gallery, New York **1993** *Half Lives,* Royal Photographic Society, Bath; *Living Room 2/Documentary,* The Museum for Photography, Braunscheweig, Germany; *Natural Resources,* Mark Boote Gallery, New York **1994** *Other Edens,* The Photographers' Gallery, London and New York **1995** The Wedding Gallerie Fotohof, Salzburg and Copenhagen.

GROUP EXHIBITIONS: **1989** *Colour Work,* Photographers' Gallery, London **1990** *Relative Values,* Centre for Creative Photography, Houston **1991** *Enter the Others,* Strasbourg **1992** *Nenos,* The Vigo Photography Centre, Spain; *Enter the Others 2,* Lisbon, Portugal; *Our Town Burden,* Gallery, New York **1993** *Aperture 40th Anniversary Exhibition,* Burden Gallery, New York; *About Big Cities,* Neue Gesellschaft, Berlin; *Air,* Alexander Kunsthalle, Rotterdam; *Montpelier Photography Festival,* Montpelier; *Krieg,* Neue Galerie, Gratz **1994** *Whose Looking at the Family?,* Barbican Art Gallery, London **1995** *The Dead,* National Museum of Photography, Bradford; *After the Sublime,* Cambridge Darkroom.

LIST OF EXHIBITS

Adam Beebee
Ultras 1995
acrylic on canvas
66 each 15 x 15cms
installation 49 x 372cms

Roderick Buchanan
Work in Progress 1993-4
mounted and laminated colour photographs on
wooden ledge
39 each 50 x 40cms
dimensions variable

New commission
Roderick Buchanan
Ten in a Million 1994-6
Manchester (Glasgow, Budapest, Amsterdam,
Nantes, Berlin and New York)
video presentation
4 each 20mins (played continuously)

New commission
Freddy Contreras
Stud 1996
11 x pairs of shoes fitted with studs
dimensions variable

Rosana Fuertes
Pasión de multitudes 1992-3
acrylic on board
39 pieces each 20 x 22cms
dimensions variable

ew commission
ucy Gunning
he Footballers 1996
ideo presentation on surveillance monitor

ew commission
rispin Jones
aptain Nevill 1996
nounted and laminated colour photograph and
ext panel
05 x 100cms

New commission
abriel Kuri
Untitled 1996
rinted adhesive labels and found objects
imensions variable

Simon Patterson
*The Last Supper Arranged According to the
Sweeper Formation (Jesus Christ in Goal)* 1990
acrylic paint on gallery wall
limensions variable

Simon Patterson
*The Last Supper Arranged According to the Flat
Back Four Formation (Jesus Christ in Goal)* 1990
acrylic paint on gallery wall
limensions variable

New commission
Nathalie Turner
Bet I Finish My Sticker Book Before You **1996**
colour feltpen on self-adhesive labels
approx 300 each 10 x 6cms
installation lengths 4 x 340cms

New commission
Martin Vincent and David Mackintosh
*Bundesliga (One World Cup and Two World
Wars...)* 1996
video presentation on wall-mounted monitor
90mins (played continuously)

New commission
Mark Wallinger
vs. 1996
carbon on paper
22 various sizes

New commission
Mark Wallinger
Man United 1996
knitted wool
dimensions variable

New commission
Nick Waplington
Best of British 1996
c-type colour photographs
4 each 180 x 120cms

Catalogue published by Manchester City Art Galleries and the Institute of International Visual Arts for the exhibition

OFFSIDE!
Contemporary Artists and Football

Manchester City Art Galleries
8 June - 1 September 1996

Exhibition organised by Manchester City Art Galleries in collaboration with the Institute of International Visual Arts. Curated by John Gill

Exhibition Co-ordinators, Manchester City Art Galleries:
Tim Wilcox and Howard Smith

Exhibition Co-ordinators, InIVA:
Gilane Tawadros and David Chandler
assisted by Victoria Clarke
Press: Nick Hallam

Catalogue designed by Chrissie Morgan
Edited by Tim Wilcox

Printed by Jackson Wilson Printers Ltd., Leeds

ISBN 0 901673 50 1

Cover: Lucy Gunning *The Footballers*
Back cover: Crispin Jones *Captain Nevill* (detail)

The Contributors

John Gill is a freelance curator who previously worked as Curator of Exhibitions, Royal Festival Hall Galleries. His most recent exhibition was BOXER for Walsall Museum and Art Gallery. He is currently co-ordinator of the South East Exhibitions Project, an exhibitions development service initiated by South East Arts.

Simon Kuper is the author of *Football Against the Enemy* which won the William Hill Sports Book of the Year Award. He now works for the *Financial Times.*

Richard Williams writes for *The Guardian* and is the author of *The Death of Ayrton Senna.*